Praise for *Lo-Fi Citadels*

"Andrew Collard brings the eye of a naturalist to these poems—if by nature one might consider the post-industrial urban and suburban landscapes where all the forces of commerce and culture come to bear on human relationships and the individual imagination. Whether considering 'love as American as a shutoff notice,' or 'the strongholds / we've established among the asphalt's interludes,' Collard refuses to see the personal as disconnected from the places and forces that give it shape. This is an important book and one I'll be reading for many years to come."

—David Hornibrook, author of *Night Manual* (Wayne State University Press)

"In *Lo-Fi Citadels*, Andrew Collard actively constructs a rugged landscape of American tenderness and collapse—where grocery aisles, flooded freeways, and the hum of late-night Motown become the scaffolding of survival. These poems move through Michigan's post-industrial landscapes with a steady ache for connection, asking what remains when literal and figurative infrastructures fail, particularly in a contemporary wasteland degraded by late-stage capitalism and sociopolitical unrest. Collard writes, 'ours is a love as American as a shutoff notice,' stark commentary on individual economies in our country—there is little return in investment of what we give and give and give of ourselves. His formal inventiveness and lyricism hums with radio interference, tuning into the frequencies of fatherhood, class, labor, and loss. *Lo-Fi Citadels* is both elegy and anthem—a mixtape of endurance where the everyday is mythic and ruin is radiant."

—Iliana Rocha, author of *The Many Deaths of Inocencio Rodriguez*

"'I see something I want you to see,' writes Andrew Collard in 'Bus Stop Promenade.' What he sees are the people who are often unseen: commuters, custodians, and cashiers, those whose lives are 'as American as a shutoff notice.' Collard also hears something he wants us to hear—music and the 'current of sound' in our daily lives—while warning us of the siren's call of consumerism, the 'amplifier / for ideas that someone else wants [us] thinking of.' *Lo-Fi Citadels* is a glorious mixtape of precarity and pleasure. You will want to read it on repeat."

—Erin Murphy, author of *Human Resources* and editor of *The Book of Jobs: Poems About Work*

"In this visionary collection, Andrew Collard is on high alert, pulling in wild, scattered images into thrumming riffs that keep us alive in a world that rarely recognizes us. You too will read these brilliant lines aloud to someone you love and dance the unlikely dances."

—Jim Daniels, author of *Late Invocation for Magic: New and Selected Poems*

LO-FI CITADELS

Made in Michigan Writers Series

A complete listing of the books in this series can be found online at wsupress.wayne.edu.

LO-FI CITADELS

Poems by Andrew Collard

WAYNE STATE UNIVERSITY PRESS
DETROIT

ISBN 9780814353103 (paperback)
ISBN 9780814353110 (ebook)

Library of Congress Control Number: 2025945081

Cover design by Tracy Cox

Publication of this book was made possible by a generous gift from The Meijer Foundation.

Wayne State University Press rests on Waawiyaataanong, also referred to as Detroit, the ancestral and contemporary homeland of the Three Fires Confederacy. These sovereign lands were granted by the Ojibwe, Odawa, Potawatomi, and Wyandot Nations, in 1807, through the Treaty of Detroit. Wayne State University Press affirms Indigenous sovereignty and honors all tribes with a connection to Detroit. With our Native neighbors, the press works to advance educational equity and promote a better future for the earth and all people.

Wayne State University Press
Leonard N. Simons Building
4809 Woodward Avenue
Detroit, Michigan 48201-1309

Visit us online at wsupress.wayne.edu.

CONTENTS

LO-FI CITADELS

(*Track 1*)

Now that I have been estranged from them, the corridors and signals
of the grid seem little more than an intrusion on the landscape

and the people commuting through it, like a bar band stumbling
through "Superstition" before a captive audience of waitstaff. It's raining

in the suburbs, in the city, the ditches and imaginary borders between,
and tonight, the spirit of confusion descending on them demands of me

a recounting of their surfaces and gestures, a private map that might
make sense of all the pieces: There's you, huddled above the street

in your secret citadel composed of vinyl records and newsprint,
and here's me, curbside, like a survivor of some eliminated timeline,

dispatched by you, my lover, on an unlikely mission to the grocery store
for blackberries. Toward the cruiser idling in the corner of the lot

I whisper *false earth*, toward the shopping cart and the invisible sicknesses
encircling us, *false earth*, but to acknowledge the face of the machine

we are caught in doesn't change a thing: We are irradiated by nine-to-five,
irradiated by broadcast and infrastructure. How to get in somewhere

before the cold comes is the game I've always been unconsciously
squandering my quarters in, and maybe it's the crowd of strangers milling

before the register with their bags of Technicolor peppers and gallon jugs,
or maybe it's the long aisle leading me back out into the catastrophe

of Wednesday evening, but once I think to look for them, the strongholds
we've established among the asphalt's interludes reveal themselves

as everywhere: the park bench where you swear you got me drunk on wine
the week we met, which I remember nothing of but still accept as canon,

the house you used to rent where, one incandescent Saturday, we found
compelling reasons to stay in. These fictions we are growing to inhabit

aren't less sincere than any other, than the grid itself, sustained thus far
on a calamity of motion. Here, in our obsolescence, we are revised endlessly

like a taped-over video cassette, and, Love, at the first break in the weather,
I will return with as many blackberries as our dead tech frames can hold.

THE COLLECTED INTERLUDES

BUS STOP PROMENADE

it's not as if I chose it   this bag of organs   I carry badly or so I think
before the crowd   of watchful laborers and joggers   congregating
at the bus stop   I have lips don't I   have eyelashes long enough to notice
innuendo   I have legs a beloved   might tie into knots one day
if only I would let them   the man that I first built   of these materials
was buzzing radio and clementine   the way I walked was much
too loud   my speaking voice a wisp I mangled   in order to continue
comprehensible   O the things I do to body   O stone smoothed
by its descent through time   tell the street-side inquisition   that desire
has so little for me   to do with rut with root   tell the gargoyles
in the fountain   that what I know of my own life   is only memory
and conjecture   once we're loosed from   all those ancient
conversations   about what body means   we get to fuck it up again
I have thighs don't I   have collarbones   that some nights call out
for a stranger's tongue   from here   among stray nods and glances
the entire continent of me   rolls and stretches   ornamenting nowhere
without narrative without praise   from here   before my own reflection
in the transit station window   I see something   I want you to see

FOR THE PIANIST ON SMOKE BREAK OUTSIDE THE GRAND RAPIDS BALLET COMPANY

In a corps, it matters less whose steps are whose, but, still,

a dissonance among them can unravel

the whole of the performance. Tonight, my little ballerino

doesn't feel too much like dancing,

I can tell: This style of movement, also, is syntax,

and he constructs it even as his thoughts

are elsewhere, never wants to skip. If the countryside

is consumed with water, he dances.

If the routes we take are too scabbed over with work crews

to pass, he dances. It isn't the vaguely

distant payoff of recital that compels him but *presence*:

the director's instructions echoing

above the piano, the tunes you shuffle nimbly through,

measures branching, the dancers

and their weekly repetitions of the shift to first position

or to second. To call it holy would be

to disregard how casual this practice is, how plain,

and anyway, I have grown tired

of holiness. The argument over what must be preserved

as sacred and by whom will burn on

without us like a wildfire of obscure origin, while loosed

children play chase in the lobby between

the minute the advanced class ends and theirs begins,

one finishing his bag of fries, another

slumped against his mother, not unhappily, running fingers

through a carpet whose texture always

will return him here, this surface of an unfamiliar world.

NOCTURNE WITH VACANT LOT

the wooden fence of the yard behind us
meant to keep the wild out

was overtaken again by vines
reaching their forearms

across the weathered expanse
toward each other

if only to know for sure
against the widening hush

that something else
along the earth was growing—

AUBADE WHERE THINGS ARE PRETTY GOOD ACTUALLY

The idea that every fallen leaf is not unique,
        reduced into a name like *maple*
and understood as simple variation on a theme,
        is just a trick of speaking—
in the swollen morning after love, there is space
        in my attention for every *oak* and *birch*,
each seed carried off by the particulars of an hour
        no one foresaw. It was want
that woke us, pounding like driftwood caught
        inside a current, it was want
that baffled all those categories hounding us
        from safe house to safe house
through the suburbs of gender. Now, I am no one's
        dataset, and the billboard models
posing along the length of the commute seem
        too open-mouthed for good taste—
and tell me, is there anything as indecent as an elevator,
        its rise and drop, doors sliding
to release us as though heavy with our whispering?
        It's part recall, part fact of you
that drapes me gently up against the offices
        on Main Street: in my shoulders,
in my calves, I bear the evidence, in motion
        and at rest. There is no parting,
and from here all possible routes through afternoon
        meander back toward the same
inverted skyline of you and me, the ceiling fan,
        and dried-up globs of paint. Even
the most intensely felt of absences is sequential—
        now you see us, now you don't—
and wherever it is I go to after, I carry with me
        all the instances I've been
composed of: once, the heavy metal taste of you
        along my teeth, once, your breath
against the collar of my mostly buttoned shirt.

FIT CHECK

Define *uniform*: coveralls, dress blues, apron with pockets

functionally useless. Our bravest face, our gladiator drag,

secondhand khakis and a golf shirt stitched with the corporate

insignia of FYE or Cold Stone. Every day told to be decent, to lose

our shapes inside of what we didn't ask for, selling movies,

serving food or cooking it, assembling a car we couldn't afford

even with our discount, clad in bow ties, straight ties, nylons,

our scrubs in assorted shades. Somehow, we manage to make it

look so good, the broken-heel best intention, the scuffed jean

and secret hole-ridden sock we don as if in protest of

the daily masquerade. We clear away the leaves, scatter sawdust

on the schoolroom floor, strutting in our worst vest, bodice,

government-issue coat, embroidered. This, our first recital,

game face, our cover song pitched for someone else's range,

the title that was never ours to which we must respond—

an inheritance, the disquiet that inhabits us by dawn or later,

postshift, returning to find our children sunk already into sleep.

MONSTER MOVIE

(After Ishirō Honda)

—It starts with a chipped-at fishing boat //
a model // my uncle set adrift //
                [DISSOLVE]   atop a dresser //
after *ghosting* // after *headphones will protect me* //
after *mother*
                    —[MATCH CUT] It starts
with my closed-fisted // child //
breathing new //
                          & our disinvited uncle
nonetheless transpiring // in the waiting room

[INSERT] a too-expensive fire truck
for too-small baby // my sweet son // busy learning
light
      —[B-ROLL] It starts with a shadowed figure
stalking bombed-out homes //
                                        wearied soldiers
mobilizing in an unlit city // tanks & ray guns //
all anticipation // sirens // like a storm
always dispersing //
                              —It starts
where no conflict is apparent // [LONG TAKE]

television beaming
& innocuous // a secondhand couch //
                                                child clinging
to my shirt // the way I once did
to a man   who felt his blood so eloquent
he demanded my forgiveness //
                                          threat smoldering
in his absence //   while on-screen [REVERSE SHOT]
a creature // lost in an age of correspondence
rages // & stomps whole
                                  city blocks to dust

AUTOTOPIA

(Sterling Heights, Michigan)

I bet you thought I wouldn't notice the sound of fighter jets

from behind the cloud cover, the armored transport housed
inside the city garage, gas mask on its seat. There is a passive voice

to grind the edges off the story of almost anything that's happened,
there are signs and wonders biblical in scope,

                                   and I am still here, maneuvering

like a robin in a bag of grass. Autotopia, your boulevard is an amplifier
for ideas that someone else wants me thinking of: which bank

to give my checks to, the virtue of a well-kept yard. Despite the halls
filled with rival Protestants on either corner of the intersection,

despite the fire hose of information and all the news fit for cinema

disrupting every line of questioning, there is nothing, nothing
that can eradicate the alley of night rolling over me, that stillness

                                   where I can see most clearly what I am,

the process I'm entrapped by. It happens in traffic where we wait
like coaster riders stranded upside down for hours before rescue,

it happens in the field that used to be a school behind the pub:
Whatever intelligence I lay claim to is inseparable from my breathing

and the organs that sustain it. If the machine of me goes off script
and beyond your ability to improvise, what then? Autotopia,

you express yourself most genuinely through misdirection and avoidance:

The armed guard outside the pharmacy isn't there for my protection,
and the fourteen varieties of gum before the counter are all just gum.

DISASTER GROCERY

The paid shopper casing the aisle of frozen
entrées has, it seems, discovered that the secret
to his heart's content has taken the form of precooked
sausage links, never to be procured, the shelves of
Wealthy Market nearly bare. Another Wednesday
morning that can't decide what it wants to be,
on the hundredth anniversary of the last time
that anyone touched me, and for better or
for nothing I have fled the safety of my home,
from its dirt-floor basement and slightly running water
to citrus, to candy, to whatever my Bridge Card
will allow, and yes, please, Mr. Greeter, I would
like some tape to stand on (*this way, sir*), and yes
please, Mr. Page, I would like to be reminded,
kindly, not to touch my face. This is not
The Odyssey, I know, and should the gods wish
to punish me, they'll have to follow, to their shame,
on foot. It's April in Michigan, the republic
of engine blocks, in the epoch of the pink slip,
and I am without a car, April in Michigan,
and you'd think by now everything that could've
passed on would have, the drooped vines, branches,
whatever it's called, the stuff you burn to start
a longer burn that gathers in the corners of
the yards (*brush*), along the fences I trace back home
with my bagful of astonishments, the stillness struck
by just enough commotion that I might be fooled
into believing that the worst is over, finches
dodging between the sprouts of wild geraniums
and Queen Anne's lace, so cheap here, pushing
through the earth into a cold that has no cure.

TO MY SON HENRY, AFTER A MOVIE

Hyper laundry. Ultra commute. In our living room,
there's a planet where the golden age of robots

and dinosaurs continues on. I have learned
to draw strength from plastic fortresses, the saga

unfolding in their midst. In our latest matinee,
after battling a kitchen chair, our hero

Ghidorah, the Three-Headed Monster, ventures
too close to a black hole and is lost in space. He drifts

through a darkened universe of charged particles
and gas giants where gravity is so severe that no one

escapes their skies. Before your arrival, O astronaut,
there was a cracked LP in me repeating scraps

of sound I could not make sense of, and for years
I lived inside the ruckus: an empty drone

I mistook for everything. This soundtrack of the void
is only ominous until we understand its tortured

waveforms were not meant for us, rendered only
with our best guess and data. From the right altitude,

our neighbors, the traffic on Leonard Street, the oaks
look like miniatures and figures, the driveways

like stones riprapping a path for Ghidorah as he strides
toward the crowded square where monster friend

and robot alike—everyone he loves—have assembled
to welcome him back into the city of tomorrow.

LATE BULLETIN

Facts scatter before me like debris from an airplane I must reassemble
in order to divine a port of origin—

Item: Coyotes have made their way south into the city.
Item: My son's clothes have become a size too small.

I am thinking of the spaces between us all and how we fill them,
this song of love we call *economy*, moving cautiously to work

to home to shopping in our city of weekend visitors.

Item: Woman sets fire to house while destroying bedbugs.
Item: My phone is pulsing on the table.

By the time news of the high court's ruling is handed down
and screens citywide begin to flare with commentary and statistics,

I am crying on a couch, surrounded by the only photos I still have

of a friend I've learned I'll never see again—
curtains of distance, curtains of narrative obscuring

anything that might explain his sudden absence.

Still, the hours send us on our errands: I dial a distracted
phone call here and poke the stray elevator there.

The local soliloquies by bus stop, pastry counter, and linen factory
ramble on unwritten, my glass slips from the counter, the wildfire

and flood roll on, the austerity, the estrangement—
ours is a love as American as a shutoff notice.

ROGERS PLAZA ETUDE

Behold, the secondhand embarrassment
of the palace that can't retain its tenants,
the holes in the arrangement, marked FOR LEASE,
where once an OfficeMax or Kroger might
have presided above the commons. I'm afraid
you've come too late for anything except
overstock: a malfunctioning TV or
the jersey of a bum the Tigers traded
years behind. The letters on the storefront
windows stand for something, only
now it's somewhere else, in the file cabinet
of a distant headquarters, a decade
in the century before this one. Still,
despite the empty space, there are reasons
to come here, a post office branch sometimes
drawing crowds on Saturday, the salon
whose drywall has been, again, repainted
as if to assure you these wings are not
forbidden. If I can make you need me
first, then maybe one day you could learn
to love the way the morning sun blasts through
the panels in my ceiling and the scent
of popcorn radiates from the vendor's
final stand. Not everything is so absent
as the play set resembling breakfast food
the kids once tumbled from. I was carried
to this place in pieces and will leave it
just the same, incapable of simple
services or transactions: *Come dancing*,
the Kinks plead before the gated entrance,
come in from the rain, I mean to tell you,
sticker across my lock signaling WELCOME.

AUBADE WITH MR. COFFEE AND COMMUTE

for an animal   even as simple as us to happen
everything must go right   the proper elements

and uninterrupted swaths of time   endured alone
it is the same for every object   random as a *scarf*

the necessary parts first harvested   then freighted
over depth and surface   this is why at 7:00 a.m.

we are awake   with important papers arranged
across a cast-off desk   turns out we are capable

though no one else seems to think so   the shower's
temperature is scalding   and the towels smell nice

and the leak in Mr. Coffee   doesn't spoil a thing
it's just spilled water   that will face its irrelevance

with a kind of dignity   I am carrying these latent
thoughts of you   along the morning's tributaries

into the immediacy   of what we all agree is spring
to unpack the archive of my hips   and practice

how to hold them   now that you've finally taught me
to unearth their embarrassment   of particular riches

I am whispering to myself *open*   I am thinking *tulips*
there is still some stray talk   of destiny and prayer

along the kingdom of the privacy fence   but for now
it's only talk   at this early hour the light can seem

one way to me   then suddenly can seem another
and in that window of transition   I sometimes think

the conditions for our happiness   might acquiesce with us
arms flung wide like maple branches   over the commute

to once and always tell me what I want   is not impossible

LO-FI CITADELS

(Track 2)

The bridge to anywhere is out, the freeway closed for repairs,

the Wi-Fi signal shoddy, the phone broken. There is no body,

no avenue through which you might receive what you imagine

to be your beloved's manifestos of longing, every dialogue

a fragment. The money shadow has begun to replicate

in your chest, your hips, the usual locales you freight worry with

back into your living-room life, your spraying-down-the-counters

life, your thermostat-adjusting, sour-coffee life. Your fingers

ache before the absence of a lover's elbow, the scruff

of hair between shoulders, these distances that some insist

are meaningless grown tangible. If you fill the space with sound,

say the Vandellas or the Shondells, if you feel the music

hard enough, the conflicted voices within you assigning blame

will disperse like a plague of grackles. Maybe you don't love

who you're supposed to. Maybe you can't make sense of your plain

old hands, your wrong shade of lips that purse as the beat gives way

to the hook. Nothing will happen, the good kind: There is no one to pardon here in your bread-bag life, your worn-carpet life,

your pencil-markings-in-a-paperback life. You are riding

vibrations from elsewhere into whatever the next hour

will bring you, dryer still tossing tomorrow's shirt, succulents

wavering from their makeshift cart in strange and perfect health.

AUTOTOPIA

THE NEIGHBORHOOD ONLY RETURNS IN FRAGMENTS

Robin, ryegrass, trilevel, oak. As though a scene enshrined
as the subject of some great painting has come up missing

and what remains is just a series of impressions. A hand
pressed to a stranger's shoulder, almost embarrassed to be felt,

and what happens after: Every day I must traverse my own
memory like a suburb full of awful roads while knowing

the patterns were arranged this way to serve another's interest.
It all gets harder to believe in, the more I embellish, dressing up

the holes between the scent of skunk, the silent evergreens,
with junk words like *there was*, *as in*, *because*, the bits that freight

the plot into a strained cohesion. Who is it now that's speaking,
and are you sure? The distance from my stories to their inception

is increasing, each an unmanned probe whose transmission
will one day cease, wandering in a night beyond all understanding.

Once upon a time, someone says, and immediately we begin
to build ourselves a habitable space inside their rhetoric,

a still life of perennials and garbage bins. O child, with autumn
jacket hanging off the stoop, the voice of disjunction has arrived

to shout down all the sense you've made of things. To preserve
these hours the way you see them now, you must invent a language

as inevitable as all that would unravel them: Your jeans are Levi's.
The stray cat is a tabby. The chalk house you've inscribed into the walk

is ornamenting concrete that the winter will reduce to rubble.

CICADA SONG

the cicadas' curtain
of unrest descends
from the backyard's

maples as if
little men were building
homes there

in the branches—

the stairs groan
beneath my father's
steps and wake me

just enough
to watch him
pause, assured

that I'm still dreaming.

LONELINESS IN THE KEY OF SPRAWL

I do the pigeon when the chorus hits,
along a sidewalk
modeling the strange shapes

weather breaks us into, I do the jogger
and the rhododendron,
though I know you are, by this hour,

far away. There was a house here, or
there could've been,
the space hushed as an instrumental

passage in the measure of a street
wracked with expansion.
Somewhere, the water backing up

through a storm drain floods a corridor
at rush hour, seeping
into the cabins of stranded cars,

and the rhythms that have carried us
from lot to lot
these last months are swallowed.

I do the evergreen, though today it seems
I have no place
in history, I do the earwig

and the cul-de-sac, but I receive no indication
of response. Before *origin*,
before memory and the thought

of home, there are questions that go on
without me, the banality
of someone deciding what to eat

and with whom. Consider how precariously
we could live together:
you, in the bedroom above, and me,

always distracted with the idea
of coming up. We could
learn, at last, the dryer vent

and the elusive junk mail, we could scare
the neighbors all week long
inventing new, unmanageable steps

as the daylilies stashed behind the garage
explode through a season's worth
of grasping vines and branches.

AUTOTOPIA

(Grand Rapids, Michigan)

these streets are narrow enough   the cars don't get broken into
arranged in columns   like record jackets   worn away by use or want

Autotopia   I segue slowly into traffic   wondering to myself

what tenderness is left for us   among the overpasses chipped at
by another decade's rain   the streetlights' distorted reflections

in puddle and glass   we are travelers of the tenuous   hurtling

feetfirst into tributaries of sound   my son eating his breakfast
in a car seat en route   and me   as I ferry him through signage

toward the learning center   stray traces of tomorrow spilling

into space around us   a phone call too early   to be anything
but a billing reminder   the picnic tables in the park   deleted

their graffiti   the hands that built them   I am lacking speech

to package up the local barrage   the heated council meetings
corporate acquisition   of a historic paper   the words I manage

misshapen   by what I've meant them to contain   wisp of dandelion

exclusion zone   it's the scope   of what I'm not equipped to notice
that scares me most   the content machine   radiating forth

an alchemy of symbolism and shock   I walk my son into class

kiss his forehead   a moment to emerge   from the emergency
embodied   before I am again preoccupied   by messages

my deluge of receipts   I am already counting   to discern

if I can hold out through summer   knowing every stop I make
along the midway of the city   will cost me   is it our turn yet

for rumors of war   the feedback loop   the shooter loose on campus

is it our turn to lose   the hour of decision   among dishes
laundry baskets   the price of eggs   inflection point diminished

by dialogue broken off   Autotopia   I am suspended

on the threshold   drawing strength from him   my child
who so often without knowing   has led me station to station

through the fun house   this maze of faces   my every possible self

converging   interlude by interlude   I will wear his laughter
his belief   like a suit of armor   as I ascend back into road noise

this carousel of murmur   a wind   you push across your reeds

INCIDENTAL PORTRAIT

A well-kept catalog of his sleeping or his meals couldn't tell you
        when the next glass might get thrown or

a sputtering run of curses might begin to spill from him like money,

which is to say what keeps him in the present tense, with you,
        must come and go. He slumps beside the table,

frail in frame, and says one cutting of pie will do, *just a little*,

knowing well digestion's burden on the body, the same wry timbre
        with which he might dispense an anecdote of Pompeii

or the long-debated crystals he's acquired, he says, for healing.

This time, when rage takes him, he disappears inside it, into
        I don't love you, I don't love any one of you, an acre

of incoherent mumbling and one slammed fist, through a country

you have yet to recognize but suspect you may be bound for
        all the same. And in the breach, as the greatest hits tape's

worth of his relations scatter and the conversation strikes up

awkwardly to muffle him, he tapers off, a branching oak trimmed
        for the convenience of the home beneath it, then begins

to thread his gaze throughout the room, desperate for news

of where he's been and why. O house of mirrors, note the way
        he leans in, cornering the market of your sentences

as if you might know better, your intentions any less a rumor—

as if your blood weren't his. O heir, what is that awful noise
          that's crept in underneath the moaning of the vents,

as he sits across the kitchen asking after you, so affable, and gone?

MONSTER MOVIE

(The Detroit Flood, 2014)

—Brief sirens dissipate into traffic [FADE IN]
as news of the disturbance spreads // a summer
afternoon gone sour // in this remote district
of the never-ending city //
                                        —Sedans stall out
in too-deep water [INSERT] scaling the median //
Our kneecaps submerged // we follow the parade
of waders toward the parking lot // the facade //
to Buddy's Pizza //
                              —Still claustrophobic
postworkday // we know what's devouring
these human bodies [MONTAGE] isn't some creature
shrouded in mystery //
                                    but infrastructure
collapsing in real time // the weather // schoolkids
and commuters crowding // onto tables //
counters slickened //
                                 —Reinforcements come quick
[JUMP CUT] and still too late // our eyes flashing
as if in a mine shaft //
                                    We have seen this somewhere //
the cinema // the monster mash // strangers
ferried [INSERT] by vehicles built for war //
fording the deluge //
                                 —Whatever happened [GRAY SCALE]
to that dream of the winged giant // demolishing
billboards and warehouses // with a gust of breath //
These days // whether cold front or the state // true
terror enters
                    [ROLL CREDITS] through the front door

MONTAGE WITH HONDA AND SQUALL

The spare tire caked in Coke spilled back in summer
is too flat to take the full weight
of your minivan, your work jeans soaked through
at the knees and knuckles scraped. You think,
I can make the BP, and turn the engine over
because, after all, it's just a mile off
along the roadside reefs of snow,
each layer topped the shade of soot, then

flurried over clean. Is it the blood lab this time,
or the late shift at the warehouse
gesturing you out into the wound of evening,
is it a child, impatiently awaiting
for hours your arrival in the principal's office,
convinced by now one night you won't return?
The van's rattle is so severe
no steering can correct it, and after thirty

seconds of convulsing over slush and concrete,
the hands you can no longer feel
fail to answer the SUV blasting toward you
across your memory of the median—
you are suspended, then, in the tangle
of all that bewilders you, where there is
no world to be recognized beyond
the dark coast of the dash, the rubber soles

through which you've come to know the cold.
From glass to broken glass, from shuddering
to silence, you can't recall the point of impact.
Every impulse that has led you
to wreck beneath an unlit streetlight
on the fourth coldest day in a year
composed of coldest days has been
a single, fluid motion. No one is coming

to ease you from the cloth-covered seat unless
you call them, no promised Samaritan
or intervening tow's bright signal will divide
the snow squall curtaining the block unless
you reach your hand toward your phone
to raise it from a bed of broken glass as though
it is the world's last piece of bread,
put your mouth to the receiver, and speak—

WINTER SOLSTICE, LITTLE CAESAR'S ARENA

(For Cade Cunningham)

I don't recognize myself in the losing, the questions after
to be answered in the impatient
stranger's gaze. This kind of night thickens in the lungs,
accruing by second hand, by squall,
until I am abandoned to it, love poem collapsed beneath
the desperation of its lines. This is
the hour the guitarist on the corner begins to think too hard
on where the notes go and how
to stretch them as a streetcar chugs north on Woodward
almost soundlessly, sedans resigned
to passing single file on the left. In the arena, with its caverns
and a full bar every thirty paces,
the voice of the crowd is always disembodied, the game
hard to parse with all the December
pressing in like heartbreak past the metal detectors, the guards
posted before every entrance
and enormous window. How shall we speak of it?
We dive to keep the ball in bounds.
We hold tenderly the officials and swoop toward the rim.
To outlast the local weather
is an aesthetic choice—performance—the riff what makes
the good things happen, this math
of fretting mean. *The second-guessing is music too,*
the solstice says. I will stumble
all the way up the lane, if I must, to get back on the board.

AUTOTOPIA

(Royal Oak, Michigan)

The street names would deflect off a stranger, but still, I must insist
upon their cadence: Greenfield, Fourteen Mile, Woodward south

    bypassing limit after city limit by Tempo, by Caravan,

the corridors of storefront, the intersections imposing order
on the loam. Autotopia, unseen capital of steel and automation,

    you are calling me back into the rhythms that produced me,

the conveyor belts, fast food, the hospital tower where I was born
and its shadow, the province of *tool and die*. You are so cloaked

    by public life it can be difficult to illustrate your scope,

the scaled-up capacities and disasters, the corporate speak
leaching into conversation to explain away how human error

    is multiplied, even as the human is displaced. What is it

you are building from the unresolved noise of the past—
these concrete stanzas, startling in their efficiency, that correct

    our every movement into use? The cars putter along

their assigned tracks from office to station to repair shop, blasting
exhaust over walls and bridges that can no longer hold together,

    materials flaked away like too-dry skin. Autotopia,

this is a resolution to speak less sensibly: I am destroyed minute
by minute on waves of anatomy, hip twinge, sickened

cells dividing without logic or approval. The microplastics

lurking in my blood laugh at the arbitrary lines you have inscribed
along the earth, your careful phrasing, the borders necessary

to sustain you, your empire of diminishing return.

AUBADE WITH BORROWED SUGAR

The ants
have made their way

through sidewalk

fissures
to the sweetness

of a melted caramel

and no one can
accuse them

of being wrong

COFFEE TRUCK

(*Exploded View*)

Note the stranger fidgeting with his coat
along the courtyard's gravel, the hesitance
with which he stows his private disasters away
in expectation of his turn before the window,
movements slow as though to promise you
that beauty isn't useless. There is everything
at stake in the way that *iced Americano*,
by his phrasing, is kneaded into melody,
carried, if barely, along the currents battering
the seafoam green of the passenger door,
and swallowed. How long will you linger on him
in this, another perfect moment, before the meeting
you are supposed to attend in twenty minutes
begins to eat away the scenery, and you, too,
must clear your throat to face the register,
working out the proper tone and volume
to be understood against the splashing of tires?
The cashier asks *would you like to add a tip*
and the customer holds two fingers up,
as in *two dollars*, as in *peace*, each holding
their breath as if to conceal it from the other,
and just as quickly as you've noticed them,
they're gone, and nobody will ever know.

POSSIBILITY MACHINE

(For Henry, age nine)

There are forces weighing down on us
beyond our ability to describe them,
but, heroically or not, we try:
One day, the school up the street burns
and Staroid, guardian of the multiverse,
glides among the ruins in search
of missing friends. Another day,
the landlord serves notice our rent

is being raised, and Hubo the Science Bot
configures his possibility machine
to catalog every method of rescue
we have yet to imagine. My kid, my king,
I think I will never be able to stop myself
from speaking to my idea of you
in the language of these stories
we've constructed out of downtime

and secondhand plastic. It is a voice
I have eased into even this afternoon,
as an online ad for housing better suited
to our epics was revealed as a scam
on our arrival before a stranger's
long-sold duplex. From universe to universe
we continue our search for spare rooms
among the leftover dust of planets. I know

there is very little evidence in the galaxy
of anything that has ever lived,
but I know, too, somewhere in hypertime,
there is a laboratory in a house
we called our own on Sigsbee Street
where the Darkspacer is hard at work
plotting the resurrection of all things
in your dresser's bottom drawer.

LO-FI CITADELS

(Track 3)

When I am reminded most acutely the streets
were devised by men
who haven't lived here, I look to the immediate

for refuge, the mulberries
my soles stomp from yard to stoop, the window
my son likes to contemplate

the soap opera of the block through. In my earbuds,
it is 1964: Martha Reeves
is taping "Nowhere to Run" in a Detroit basement,

her voice piped to the attic
for the echo. *Inventive,* we might call this,
like the snow chains arranged

over the track as percussion, but in the moment
it was what it was, lo-fi
adornment guided by necessity. On my desk,

it is 1995: The baseball cards
my son uncovered in the closet are fragile monuments
to people with fantastic names

like *Fryman* and *Fielder.* The ones with errors
in the print run are always
worth the most, imperfect renderings that no one

planned on or chose. It's from
the likes of these I reconstruct myself, the records
conveying a stranger's yearning

from one revision to another in the process
we call *history*, the ephemeral,
my son's voice alerting me to fourteen birds

assembled on the drive. The way
something always leaks in to populate the nothing
is everything: a bright gash

of color in the morning sky, the overgrown
grasses and shrubs of the tract
that no one on the block can prove they own.

SH-BOOM

AUBADE WITH BRAVE STRANGERS

I don't believe in another life
after disaster, no square one
to return to. Hurt happens,

and it is accepted into the reaction
of chemicals bearing my name,
transformed. If I seem skeptical

of love, it is only in self-defense:
I've been wishing my whole life
for just one person to be gentle

and clear with me the way you are
when you press your arms to mine
to tell me I am wanted

more of. Never was a wine-stained
glass better suited to a nightstand
than is yours this morning,

purpling shards of light by the window,
never has anyone's jumpsuit
splayed so suggestively across

a wooden chair. I am not holding you
how I thought I might months back
when we were just brave strangers

in an elevator, inventing for ourselves
the idea of the chance encounter
and all that it is capable

of unsettling. It isn't just us the city
that prepares to carry us away
has found awake: See the lilacs

wafting up before the corner bar,
                    the maples standing at attention
          before they're decent. Interval

by stolen interval, we have been
                    refined. Your shoulder bared
          above the feather comforter

is a spoke the minutes are revolving
                    on. Your hand is the place
          where elegies come to die.

THE FACT OF A BODY

Remembered it a fire escape
we met on, one window removed
from someone's kitchen, our assembled friends

coalescing into *crowd*—
remembered it a desert, and you
the only other traveler to be found there,

scorched by circumstance.

Perhaps you won't agree. You might say
it was a bus stop we met before,
an elevator, your or my eyes welling in the enormity

of what we'd each survived,
you might say we were *hinge*,
the middle eight of a forgotten single—

halcyon days overheard

as anecdote before the jukebox.
This space of waiting between
meaningful encounters is tavern-like, stories

on every surface turned up.
When someone asks, I tell it like I would
a snippet of a stranger's life,

studio chatter through tape hiss—

a motel roof, salt flats, an arcade.
Whatever it was, it's true
that we were wandering, as passersby

bumbled like blood cells
through the nearest alley, congregating,
the fact of them an elsewhere by which

to place us, hip to hip,

irised on the outskirts. No matter how
I choose to abstract it, always
the feeling comes first and gathers us toward

each other, the ache familiar—
a dialogue without alphabet
we thumb awhile, caught up in the fact of a body

and a body wondered on, aloud.

MONSTER MOVIE

(*Godzilla vs. Hedorah*)

—tin cans // wrappers // soda bottles adrift
in stagnant water // this is how the monster
accrues //
                [CROSSCUT] face risen from the deep
and looming // above the coast // the parking lot //
the corroded playscape //
                                        —it has a million
points of origin // [B-ROLL] a sky obscured
by smokestacks // tailpipes of cars // bad air
seeping through a broken window // beneath
the door //
                —burning in our eyes and throats // we watch
[REACTION SHOT] faces lit faintly by stray beams
from the TV // *Godzilla vs. Hedorah* //
                                                        —my son
likes to skip the speaking parts // in his edit
[J CUT] the good monster emerges // throws down
with the evil one // the film our model //
                                                            —with action figures
we mimic the battle scenes // haymaker [WIPE]
tail hit [WIPE] atomic blast [WIPE] // but you can't
fistfight a chemical spill // or the corporation
responsible // exhaust //
                                        [CLOSE-UP] the skin between
my fingers turns scaley // platelets leaking through //
until the wind changes // I am eroding
back into my base materials //
                                                —across the city
the monster crawls ashore [TRACKING SHOT]
becomes engorged // swallowing tanks and soldiers //

it accepts our death rays as tribute //
                                                            and even so
we beg to look away // wondering [DISSOLVE]
if our shrine of manufactured
                                                    heroes can survive

ANTIHEROIC COUPLET

to bypass the force field I was born with
you must open up the wound inside me

ONLY VISITING THIS PLANET

(For KC, 1967–2021)

Consider all that has eluded him, the souvenirs he couldn't take:
    plastic night light bearing the face of Christ,
signed baseball of a team that's best remembered for their losing.
    Consider what this does to us, navigating
the artifacts he's left as proof of having lived. There is a phone
    ringing inside my mind it is no longer possible
to answer, a sound I often have mistaken for a siren. I am expecting
    more of this, like a cold front that materializes

above us and descends. Whoever stashed this incoherent
    thrum of love with me deserves a talking to,
this snuffbox brimming with bad ideas and decisions made
    in wavering faith. Consider the brick he rescued
from the Hudson's implosion site, the Sega Genesis he barely played,
    the couple-few thousand CDs and cassettes,
consider once more those lost dogs, those resurrection bands,
    and hold them close, before they grow defunct.

DANCING SLOW

no calendar will claim us   no method   among the warehouses
we rendezvous   vintage jukebox   in our borrowed room's

corner almost   sputtering to life   off the electric charge of us

relearning to inhabit   the same shared space   this is no rite
no holy day   just the first time in a while   your mouth's on mine

the same old problem   of how to train   my out-of-practice lip

to pronounce   the way I need for touch   the first one is a note
we improvise away from and return to   while outside us   the AC's

gentle commotion   and the breathing of traffic continues   I can feel

the feeling between us   take over   no longer an *exposed nerve*
alone in my wave band   the possibility of contact   itself becomes

a kind of contact   the good-night variations   carrying us then

beyond intention   and back into our tissues   any moment
in the poem is right to volta   any rhythm we fall into   we remake

classic Motown   garage rock forty-five   the lyric rush

with my ear against your chest   I hear it building   the entire earth
vibrates and we aren't simply on it   I trace you   your arrival

into the present tense   like moon coming sudden   through a cloud

NATIONAL CONEY ISLAND

(Royal Oak, Michigan)

Hung lights seem to plunge like skyscrapers in reverse
above each booth and table, radiating as if my meal

were lit by a captive city fashioned from every noon
I've whiled here, stray warmth. At six years old, as I observed

a server scooping cheese fries on break, my father pointed
his fork and called this *heaven food*, the meal our dead

would dine on in the presence of the Lord. Imagine me
and being young enough to know, then, it was true. What isn't

a creation myth but tells you what you're made of? To glance out
through these windows is to regard the neighborhood, the houses

snatched up by strangers and rebuilt two stories larger,
like sudden mansions stitched onto the block, and the shuttered

club next door, not familiar but familial, marquee still fixed
to signal drivers HAPPY NEW YEAR, permanently wishing.

TRACE

Where the grass is tall enough to whip
and a mailbox covered with faded stickers
lies sideways in the gravel, roadside—

where the stoplight turned to *spotlight*
as the evening fell, and the motorcyclist
disappeared beneath the belly of a teenager's

reckless Focus—a boy kneels on concrete,
pressing pencil to the page to record his statement
as an ambulance pulls away and the driver

is released back to his embarrassed parents.
Once again, the arranging of the traffic cone,
the yellow tape, the slowing at the light

to see the wreckage. Once again, the sizing up,
the litigation, and a dozen officers scrutinizing
testimony as if to scare up every last detail, the custom

of history written by the living. They say
to describe the way the driver panicked, and tried to lift
the vehicle, and cried out when his ride arrived,

how the breath test came back clean. They say
to write how quickly the cops came, how the biker's
family came and went, and about the guilt,

it seems, the driver has to live with. No one
saw the man go under but the boy, who still
can't shake the image of a man crushed into grass

and a boot protruding from beneath the car,
the boy who kneels to trace his story onto pavement—
pushing moment into *monument*—to bless the dead.

DEEP CUTS

The specter of skinned elbows—kid blood—still scrapes and tumbles
down the drive. Behind, the clicking of a baseball card on spokes,

the wash of passing cars out by the freeway like marbles rolling
off a wooden table, and the reverb of a neighborhood between.

Distance gives even the deepest cuts a context: Every bruise, every lie,
every awful thing I've ever done is bellowing from where it rests

in time, cohering like an orchestra to song. Somehow, injury turns
less severe, the way buzzing from a broken radio becomes a curtain

soothing me to sleep. Three hours in jail, or six nights in a bus station,
buried parents—the stretch of mornings after, when routine's quiet

compass only points to absence—childhood's persistent embers, too,
fall in, the way an aging tower is returned to stone. To be abandoned

once is not to be unceasingly abandoned; one cut, opened, can only
bleed so much. The body does its stitching like mourners sift

through rubble for a shard of bone, acknowledging the pangs, or
it expires and goes where broken bodies go, like crayons, back in the box.

AUTOTOPIA

(*Utica, Michigan*)

Stay hungry, the Liquor-Lotto sign says, long after
its abandonment, *stay hungry*, the cloud of mosquitos
responds behind its back
along the narrowing bank
of my very first river. I pull in off Van Dyke Ave toward
a rental counter vacant fifteen years, its storefront
holding space, now,
for only speculation. Autotopia,
the evidence of yesterday is unmistakable. What I remember
is as tenuous as what you have replaced it with: I have hit
the latest locally famous potholes,
I have ordered a Coke
alone at a bar named The Gathering Place, I have waved
to passersby come to worship among the lanes
of what was once a bowling alley
and will later return home
to my assigned drive in another city. It's easy to forget
the bluegrass, too, must migrate, that the hobby store is franchised
and headquartered in the South.
The plant full of robots
up the road constructing circuit boards for weapons didn't
come from nowhere, is not a foregone conclusion any more
than the 7-Eleven on the corner is:
There is nothing present here
that is not lost in its own transition, these once-bare lots
now flush with industry. Despite the testimony of the nails
pitched from the Video King's old marquee,
circled ominously
before the window, there was nothing wrong with following
my father through aisles of grainy VHS boxes, there was
nothing wrong with the inconvenience
of borrowing them

three at a time, of waiting twenty minutes for a pizza
one door over, in a place we could afford to be—
to simplify any lineage,
                                        even this, is to betray it.

AUBADE WHERE WE ARE CAPABLE AND WISE

The logistics of what made last night possible
would be embarrassing to detail,
but we managed, each pressing item handled
and the fallback plan arranged. We left the TV on
in the other room as if to provide cover
for these brief hours we've begun to feel

almost ashamed of detouring toward, as if
to confuse the dawn coming
to impose its phony distances between us. Honestly,
we deserve an award, we are so good at this:
The tub filled, and I watched you shave
as our playlist cross-faded into memory,

the water hushing us beneath it, then
reckless and pleading. Is it so unreasonable
to imagine I could make you coffee every morning
while you sleep late because the dog says
it's not time to get up yet, to envision us
emerging together in the spill of day

without question of where it all will lead?
When the passersby notice us
preparing to depart in my fender-bent Ford, they will
shake their heads with envy, and all the children
on the block will approach our window—
partly for our sage advice but also

just because we're fun. We've embedded
ourselves so completely into the pulsing
of the neighborhood that when our enemies scour
the sidewalks for word of us, they won't catch
a single sighting, too quickly vanished
among the factories, trilevels, and oaks.

SH-BOOM

Once I'm moving   the moving gets easier   I kick my heels out

into the space around me   the life-size monster ghost I am
the skeleton   bobbing over carpet fiber   bathroom tile

arms circulating   because it seems like they're supposed to—

he won't remember this   my son   babbling his matchbox epic
by the couch   inflections of speech   although the doctor

says his language is coming late   *Sh-Boom*   the track shuffles
over the speaker   he knows it from a film   he puts his hands up

do-do-do-do   I sweep him into the air above me   and for now

my knees   the bad spaces between bones   shuttle all of me
just fine   shoulders in the game too   doing work that won't

show up in the stat sheet   this is the process   our daily ritual
he grabs tight to my chest   for now he fits there   and we fall

into a glide unthinking   past the plaster   crumbling at the window

boxes in the closet   I never did unpack   inside me is a liver
that isn't too sick yet   and inside him   a heart that is still growing

this is our national anthem   our call-and-response   the air conditioner
beginning to soften the wall   obviously patched   our books

scattered before the table   *Sh-Boom*   I am always awakening

and always here   the music a door back to my senses   the body
a door back to my world   let's say there was a song   dear reader

that changed everything   a current of sound   you stumbled on
as if it had been waiting   for your notice   where were you

when you heard it   what did it feel like   when the word came down

ACKNOWLEDGMENTS

My thanks to the editors of the following journals, in which many of the poems for *Lo-Fi Citadels* first appeared.

Another Chicago Magazine: "Autotopia" (Royal Oak, MI), "Dancing Slow," "Fit Check," "Sh-Boom," "Winter Solstice, Little Caesar's Arena"
Blackbird: "Late Bulletin"
Copper Nickel: "Loneliness in the Key of Sprawl"
Cream City Review: "Montage with Honda and Squall"
Denver Quarterly: "Monster Movie" (After Ishirō Honda)
Diode: "Autotopia" (Grand Rapids, MI), "Rogers Plaza Etude"
Dunes Review: "Autotopia" (Utica, MI)
Kenyon Review: "Aubade Where Things Are Pretty Good Actually," "Bus Stop Promenade," "Lo-Fi Citadels" (Track 1)
The Lickety Split: "Nocturne with Vacant Lot"
Los Angeles Review: "For the Pianist on Smoke Break Outside the Grand Rapids Ballet Company"
The MacGuffin: "Coffee Truck (Exploded View)," "National Coney Island," "To My Son Henry, After a Movie"
North American Review: "Incidental Portrait"
Prairie Schooner: "Disaster Grocery"
Sixth Finch: "Autotopia" (Sterling Heights, MI), "Lo-Fi Citadels" (Track 2)
Southeast Review: "The Neighborhood Only Returns in Fragments"
Vinyl Poetry: "Trace"
Waxwing: "Aubade with Mr. Coffee and Commute"
West Review: "Deep Cuts"

My thanks also to the following people, without whom this book would not exist: Deborah Augustin, Karalyn Bell, Henry Collard, the Collard fam, Emily Daniel, Nancy Eimers, Kendra Flournoy, A. M. Goodhart, Sarah Green, Cody Greene, Dennis Hinrichsen, Edward Haworth Hoeppner, David Hornibrook, Alyssa Jewell, Lawrence Joseph, Sara Lupita Olivares, William Olsen, Olivia Olson, Lindsay Rhean, Cuba Rhodes, Monica Rico, Iliana Rocha, Miles Smith, and Connor Yeck. Special thanks to Mr. Lampshade (i.m.) for his generous production impediments.

NOTES AND DEDICATIONS

"Monster Movie" (After Ishirō Honda) is dedicated to Dennis Hinrichsen. The monster movie poems owe their formal inspiration to his Brain Scan sequence in *This Is Where I Live I Have Nowhere Else to Go* (Off the Grid, 2020). This poem admires the film *Gojira* (by director Ishirō Honda, 1954).

"To My Son Henry, After a Movie" refers to a figure of the kaiju Ghidorah, who first appeared in the film *Ghidorah, the Three-Headed Monster* (by director Ishirō Honda, 1964). It is titled (almost) after a poem from Bob Kaufman's *Solitudes Crowded with Loneliness.*

"Rogers Plaza Etude" was written for the first indoor mall in Michigan, which as of this writing still exists outside of Grand Rapids, Michigan.

"Monster Movie" (The Detroit Flood, 2014) admires the film *Rodan* (by director Ishirō Honda, 1956).

"Aubade with Brave Strangers" is titled after the song "Brave Strangers" by Bob Seger.

"Antiheroic Couplet" is dedicated to Nathan Summers.

"Dancing Slow" is titled after the song of the same name by Martha and the Vandellas.

National Coney Island is the name of a chain of restaurants in the Detroit area.

"Sh-Boom" is dedicated to Henry Collard. The title refers to the 1954 song of the same name by the Chords.

ABOUT THE AUTHOR

Andrew Collard is a writer and teacher. His first book, *Sprawl*, won the Hollis Summers Poetry Prize and a gold medal in the 2024 Midwest Book Awards. He received a PhD from Western Michigan University and has served as a poetry editor for *Witness* and *Third Coast Magazine*. He lives with his son in Grand Rapids, Michigan.

EXPLORE THESE OTHER POETRY COLLECTIONS FROM WAYNE STATE UNIVERSITY PRESS

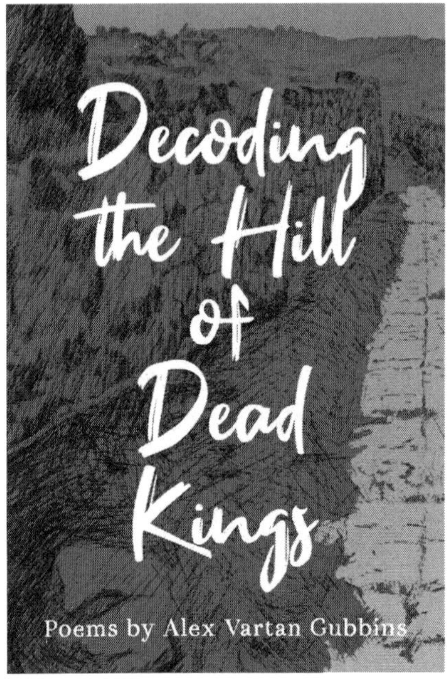

Decoding the Hill of Dead Kings

Poems by Alex Vartan Gubbins

A vivid portrait of finding home when distant places are calling.

ISBN 9780814352960, $19.99 paperback

We Live Here: Poems for an Ojibwe Calendar Year

Lois Beardslee

Foreword by Molly McGlennen

An exquisitely illustrated collection of poetry inspired by a traditional Anishinaabe seasonal year.

ISBN 9780814351468, $19.99 paperback

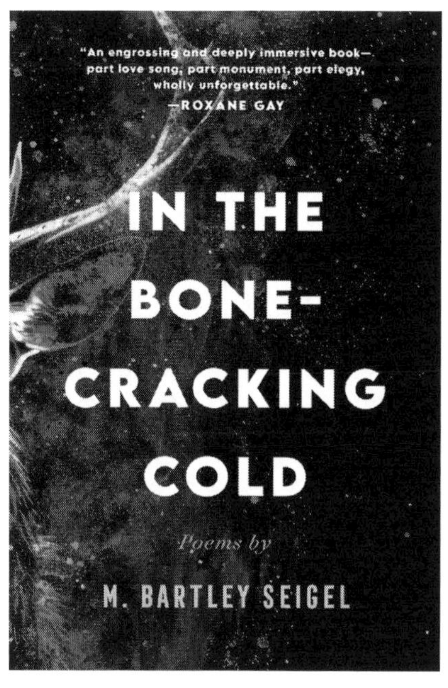

In the Bone-Cracking Cold

Poems by M. Bartley Seigel

Artfully wrought poems tracing the intimate contours of self, nature, and history.

ISBN 9780814352168, $19.99 paperback

The Lake Huron Mermaid: A Tale in Poems

Linda Nemec Foster and Anne-Marie Oomen
Illustrated by Meridith Ridl

A dazzling tale of sisterhood and the healing power of nature embodied in the Great Lakes.

ISBN 9780814347416,
$24.99 hardcover

FOR MORE INFORMATION, VISIT WSUPRESS.WAYNE.EDU.
AVAILABLE WHEREVER BOOKS ARE SOLD